CW01512470

Original title:
Rhyme Beneath the Redwood

Author: Dorian Ashford
ISBN HARDBACK: 978-1-80567-434-4
ISBN PAPERBACK: 978-1-80567-733-8

Tributes to the Towering Oak

In the shade he sways, a giant of grace,
With squirrels acting like they own the place.
His branches droop low, a soft landing pad,
While birds chime in like it's all just a fad.

Acorns drop down like nature's own gold,
With hats and a beard, he's downright bold.
The leaves whisper secrets, a rustling hoot,
As if he's the king, and we're all just a troupe.

Seraphic Silence in the Shade.

Under the boughs, the cool breeze flows,
With a chair made of vines and a seat made of snows.
I sip on my drink, but wait just a sec,
A butterfly lands, what the heck?

He twirls like a dancer, without a cue,
While ants march by in a comical queue.
Each giggle from nature, a light-hearted song,
In this shady retreat, nothing feels wrong.

Whispers of the Ancient Grove

In a grove, secrets play tag in the air,
While chipmunks giggle without a care.
The trees lean in close, like they're part of the jest,
As they tickle the clouds in a well-dressed fest.

Mossy old trunks with facial hair trends,
Join in the laughter, old buddies, and friends.
A raccoon struts by in a snazzy bow tie,
"Just passing through!" he shouts with a sigh.

Echoes in the Canopy

In the canopy high, a concert unfolds,
With frogs on the mic, singing tales untold.
The laughter of leaves, a ticklish delight,
As shadows sway gently, all through the night.

A wise old owl gives a chuckle and wink,
While squirrels reminisce with a playful blink.
The jester of nature, in all his sly ways,
Keeps us all giggling for countless days.

Shadows Speak in Verse

In the shade, squirrels plan a heist,
Nuts and acorns, they'll share a slice.
But the bird's got a beak, sharp as a knife,
Pouncing on snacks, causing some strife.

The ants march in, it's quite a parade,
With tiny flags and hats they've made.
They boast of riches, but their haul's just crumbs,
Giggling away, buzzing like drums.

Harmony in the Hushed Grove

A frog croaks out a tune so grand,
Wings a-flutter, flies take a stand.
The laughter of leaves, a ticklish sound,
As they sway in rhythm, all around.

A raccoon jigs, with style and flair,
Dancing on logs without a care.
While the owls hoot melodically,
Chiming in with their own symphony.

Nature's Tapestry in the Timber

The vines are tangled, oh what a sight,
Nature's braid, done with delight.
A beetle struts in a shiny tux,
Turning heads, like he's cashing bucks.

In a cozy nook, a caterpillar sneezes,
Making butterflies laugh with such eases.
They roll on the leaves, in fits of cheer,
Not a care in the world, no sign of fear.

Flourish of Sunlit Whispers

The trees are gossiping, what a delight,
Sharing secrets in the soft sunlight.
A bunny hops by, with a goofy grin,
Wearing a flower like a crown to win.

A wind chime sings, with each gentle breeze,
Tickling the branches, making them tease.
The sun splashes gold, with festive cheer,
While the forest laughs, oh, what a year!

Whispers in the Canopy

Squirrels chatter high above,
Acorns fall like little doves.
A chipmunk steals my sandwich fast,
With tiny paws, it makes a blast.

The leaves they rustle, play a tune,
A raccoon dances 'neath the moon.
He trips on roots and takes a spill,
Then winks at me, oh what a thrill!

A crow caws out with zest and flair,
And tosses down some tree-bark hair.
It's quite a scene, this forest show,
Where critters act like stars, you know!

So if you wander through this wood,
Just laugh along, it's all quite good.
The whispers here are not profound,
Just giggles and some nuts abound!

Shadows of the Timeless Trees

Beneath the boughs, a shadow hops,
A frog in boots, it never stops.
It croaks a tune that's out of key,
Yet all the birds sing back with glee.

A stump claims fame as king of jokes,
While mushrooms giggle, oh, those folks!
A turtle joins with timeless grace,
And trips, oh no, he fell from space!

A woodpecker pens his hit parade,
On crinkly bark, he's quite charade.
Each peck resounds like laughter bright,
In this leafy land of pure delight.

So take a stroll, embrace the cheer,
In tree-clad realms, where jesters leer.
The shadows move, let laughter tease,
In this wild world of timeless trees!

Echoes of the Ancient Ones

The ancient pines, they whisper low,
"Hey, watch your step or you might go,
To trip on roots and munch on dirt,
While giggling squirrels plan dessert!"

A bear in shades lounges nearby,
With sunglasses on, he winks an eye.
He orders snacks from passing deer,
Who serve him nuts with lots of cheer!

The owl hoots twice, a wink in style,
"Life's just a laugh, so stay awhile!"
We share a joke as leaves cascade,
This merry crew, a leafy parade.

So if you seek what woods can bring,
Join in the fun, let laughter sing.
With echoes shared from sages wise,
The ancient ones deliver surprise!

Verses in the Forest's Heart

In the woods where shadows play,
A hedgehog strolls, it's quite a day.
With little hats and tiny shoes,
He bids the butterflies adieu!

A fox rehearses lines for fun,
His dramatic flair cannot be shunned.
He struts and frets, a true delight,
As rabbits giggle at his sight.

The brook hums softly, calls a tune,
With fish that dance beneath the moon.
They splash about, creating waves,
As frogs applaud from leafy graves.

So join the mirth, don't be aloof,
In this forest where we share the proof.
Of verses spun with laughter bright,
A heart of woods, a pure delight!

Ballad of the Briar and Thorn

In the woods where the briars grow,
A mischievous hare puts on a show.
He tangles his ears in the thicket tight,
And hops in circles, what a sight!

With thorns in tow, he takes a leap,
Over a creek, oh what a sweep!
But lands in a puddle, splashes all around,
While giggling to himself, he's truly profound.

He chases a squirrel, who's quick and spry,
Right up a tree, oh my oh my!
But with a flick and a twist, he misses the branch,
And down comes the hare, in quite the enhance!

Echoing Footsteps in the Wild

In the wild where echoes play,
A woodpecker starts his day.
With a tap, tap, tap on a tree so tall,
His rhythm's off, and he's bound to fall!

A turtle's trying to jog along,
But his little legs can't keep the song.
He hums a tune, so slow and sweet,
While the raccoons giggle at his slow, slow feet.

The deer all prance with graceful flair,
While the rabbits hop without a care.
Yet one little bunny trips and rolls,
And soon every creature is laughing in shoals!

Lyrical Light Through the Leaves

In a forest dense with shadows deep,
A fox sings softly, trying not to creep.
His voice is shy, a little unsure,
While the owls hoot, and start to concur!

The sunlight glimmers, playful and bright,
As squirrels join in, causing quite a fright.
They jump and tumble, with joy they weave,
And the hedgehog just sighs, "Get me out, I'll leave!"

A rabbit, well-dressed, with a tie so meek,
Stumbles on a log, let's take a peek.
He lands on his back with a thump and a bounce,
And shouts, "Next time, I'll wear something pounced!"

The Base of the Bashful Behemoths

At the base where giants loom,
A caterpillar shakes off the gloom.
He dreams of soaring, oh what a flight,
But trips on a pebble—a sad, funny sight!

The bears nearby, they chuckle loud,
As the little worm wriggles, feeling proud.
"I'll show you all, just wait and see!"
But his tiny legs are stuck, oh me, oh me!

Pinching their sides, the birds chirp on,
As the caterpillar declares, "Watch out, the dawn!"
Then off he rolls, with a flurry and flare,
And lands in a patch of daisies—oh dear, beware!

Heartbeats of the Hollowed Trunk

In a trunk so broad and round,
Squirrels play, jumping around.
They wear tiny hats, oh so dandy,
Dancing jigs, getting quite randy.

A raccoon peeks from a knothole,
Claiming this tree as his goal.
With a wink and a mischievous grin,
He hoards all the snacks — he's the kingpin.

Birds chirp tunes with voices sweet,
While ants march in a marching beat.
They form a band and sing for fun,
Under the rays of a warm, bright sun.

But watch your step near the base,
For a spider might take your place!
Giggles echo around the wood,
In this world where all is good.

Verses from the Verdant Sanctuary

Here in the park, beneath the leaves,
Even the worms wear little sleeves!
They wiggle and giggle, what a sight,
Admiring the sky, so very bright.

Bees buzz by with their busy hum,
While ladybugs drum on a tiny drum.
They team up for a fun charade,
Each spin a dance, in the forest glade.

A fox wears boots, oh so chic,
He struts and prances, what a freak!
His friends all laugh, in the shade they huddle,
As he dances the day away, in a muddle.

Under the gnarled branches, they'll cheer,
Making up jokes about each deer.
Laughter floats through the sunlit green,
A joyous tone, the happiest scene.

Tales of Twisted Trunks

A tree of wisdom twists and bends,
With branches that swoop, making friends.
A gopher pops up, wearing a tie,
Declaring this day a party to fly!

The shadows play tricks in the light,
As butterflies flirt, what a delight!
They sip from nectar, gossiping fast,
Spreading fun tales of seasons past.

The owls tell stories, swirling profound,
Of moonlit adventures, all around.
With a hoot and a wink, they take a pause,
To marvel at nature and its laws.

A good old bear starts to groove,
With a shuffle and shake, what a move!
Under the boughs, they laugh and play,
In their own little world, come what may.

Twilight's Embrace in the Trees

Squirrels in jackets dance with glee,
While owls hold court for tea,
A raccoon plays a tune on a flute,
Beneath the stars, all looking cute.

The bushes giggle as shadows grow,
Frogs in bow ties put on a show,
A sloth slips by with style, no doubt,
While crickets cheer, wiggling about.

Fireflies wink like they're in on the joke,
A deer prances in, just to provoke,
Foxes laugh as they chase their tails,
While the moon hangs low, in cozy veils.

Laughter echoes through branches wide,
As raccoon's hands slip, oh what a slide!
In twilight's grip, all fun begins,
With nature's quirks, where joy always wins.

Melodies from the Mutable Woods

Beetles tap dance on a leaf,
Each step brings jest, beyond belief,
A chipmunk croons a silly song,
As nightingale joins in, all night long.

Branches sway to a playful beat,
While shadows prance on tiny feet,
The wind chuckles, through leaves it flows,
Whispering secrets that only it knows.

A gopher plays guitar with grit,
And giggles follow every skit,
Bunnies hop, their ears a-pirouette,
In this wacky woodland minuet.

As laughter spills beneath the sky,
A hedgehog sings with a glimmer of shy,
In the heart of the forest, life's a game,
In this symphony, none are the same.

Pathways of Poetic Shadows

Mice on bicycles zoom past trees,
Making shortcuts, if you please,
A hedgehog zips right by in a hoodie,
With a look of mischief, oh so moody!

Under the ferns, shadows twirl,
Goblins bicker, while goblins hurl,
Banana peels on the quaint path spread,
For antics alive with giggles ahead!

A raccoon steals snacks with flair,
While racquets seem to float in the air,
Each critter plucking at the strings,
Creating laughter that never stings.

As dusk creeps in, the fun won't cease,
In the murmur of leaves, laughter's release,
In wooded paths, where tales unwind,
The joy of the forest, ever kind.

Musings Among the Mossy Roots

Toadstools gather for a feast,
Inviting every beast and least,
A turtle spins like a record turn,
While ladybugs laugh at the mossy churn.

Fungi sprout, with colorful flair,
While adding to the merriment in the air,
Mice with hats, so dapper and neat,
Join in a conga, a charming feat!

The owl hoots now, in rhythmic beat,
As fireflies glow, keeping time complete,
With shadows laughing, the night takes a bow,
In this whimsical world, all hearts sing "wow!"

So gather 'round for the wild midnight,
Under the stars that shine so bright,
The trees serve giggles, from trunk to root,
In nature's theater, the laughter's absolute.

The Ballad of Bark and Bristle

In the forest deep and wide,
The trees have tales they can't hide.
A squirrel sings, a woodpecker taps,
While raccoons wear their silly hats.

The branches dance, they twist and sway,
With winds that laugh and play all day.
A deer prances with a youthful boast,
While the fox claims he's the funniest host.

In shadows thick, jokes echo loud,
As ferns and fungi form the crowd.
A chipmunk cracks a nutty quip,
Turning logs into a comedy trip.

So raise a toast to the tree brigade,
Where laughter echoes, never fade.
For beneath the bark, the fun's afoot,
In nature's jest, we all take root.

Canopy Cadence

Up high where the branches play,
The giggles float like leaves in May.
A parrot squawks a silly truth,
While squirrels joke about their youth.

The sunbeams dance on mossy ground,
While owls hoot in a comical sound.
With every rustle, a chuckle springs,
As nature's choir brightly sings.

Frogs leap with a splash and a croak,
Even the trees seem to joke and poke.
The breeze tosses the laughter around,
A merry melody, a playful sound.

So swing and sway, lose your cares,
Join in the fun, for life's a affair.
Amidst the leaves, let laughter soar,
In this tall tale, forever more.

Melodies of Moss and Moonlight

In the quiet night, where shadows grow,
The luminescent dance starts to flow.
Fireflies flicker, they waltz in pairs,
While crickets compose with tiny snares.

A badger hums a forgotten tune,
Under the gaze of the sleepy moon.
With every giggle, the stars all wink,
As the night creatures begin to think.

The moose starts jiving, it's quite absurd,
While a wise old owl just observes the herd.
With each little hop, the laughter spreads,
As shadows frolic on all the beds.

In this enchanted mossy glade,
Where echoes of joy will never fade.
Let the melodies of night be known,
In every whisper, we're never alone.

Harmonies of the Hidden Glen

In a glen where secrets are kept,
The trees are giggling, while others slept.
A bunny hops in a comical race,
With a hedgehog wearing a tiny face.

The brook babbles with a cheeky sound,
As leaves jazz up the fun around.
With each splash, a story unfolds,
Of creatures bold and laughter untold.

The chattering chipmunks conduct their show,
While the shy fawn blushes, stealing the glow.
Every rustle, a whisper of cheer,
In this hidden glen, where joy is near.

So join the dance, cast worries away,
In nature's arms where we all play.
For beneath the trees, the spirit is free,
In harmonies shared, just you and me.

Nature's Nocturne in the Neath

In shadows lurk the squirrels bold,
With acorns tossed, their tales unfold.
They chatter soft, conspiracies rise,
While moonbeams dance, and laughter flies.

A raccoon dons a masked display,
As fireflies join the grand ballet.
The night is young, the fun's afoot,
In nature's show, we laugh, we hoot.

A frog in boots hops by with glee,
Singing songs of irony.
While owls wink from their lofty seats,
The forest hums with silly beats.

So gather 'round and find your cheer,
In nocturnal games, no room for fear.
For laughter thrives where wild things roam,
In midnight's hug, we find our home.

Poetry of the Pine's Embrace

Oh, how the pines sway with grace,
They tickle each other's leafy face.
A gentle breeze, they shake and shimmy,
Like dancers dressed in shades so whimsy.

The woodpecker's drum, a rhythmic beat,
Echoes joy where roots and branches meet.
Squirrels scamper, their antics wild,
In nature's play, I feel like a child.

With cones aplenty, the critters feast,\nWhile poets moan
for their rhymes, at least.
In this tall forest, fun takes flight,
Among the pines, we giggle all night.

So raise a toast to the trees so grand,
With every laugh, life takes a stand.
In this embrace of branches wide,
Let every heart be filled with pride.

Stanzas in Sunlight and Shade

A sunbeam sneezes, turns to gold,
While shadows whisper secrets told.
The daisies giggle, heads held high,
As butterflies waltz, oh my, oh my!

A bumblebee hums a bouncing tune,
While ants march round in a busy swoon.
Glimmers of laughter, rays in flight,
In this patchwork quilt, the world feels right.

The sun's warm pillow, oh what a dream,
While squirrels engage in a nutty scheme.
With every twirl of the gentle breeze,
Nature's antics are sure to please.

So join the party, don't be shy,
With every moment, let laughter fly.
In sunlight's glow or shade so deep,
Nature's jests are ours to keep!

A Sonnet for the Silent Sentinels

Tall sentinels, they stand so proud,
With knots and twists, they boast their crowd.
They keep a watch on the silly fun,
With leaves that shimmer in the sun.

The chipmunks race, a dash and dart,
Each leap they take, a work of art.
The wise old tree just rolls its eyes,
At antics played beneath the skies.

A wood frog croaks a comical tune,
As night descends, beneath the moon.
Beneath their branches, joy is found,
In laughter's echo, a sweet sound abound.

So let us gather in this grove,
Where every creature finds its trove.
In silent watch, they ease our way,
With chuckles bright, they greet the day.

Rhythms of the Wildwood

The squirrel dances with flair,
Chasing shadows without a care.
A chipmunk giggles, strikes a pose,
While wandering tales the owl knows.

The breeze whispers a sneaky tune,
As critters gather, round the moon.
A frog croaks jokes, the crowd does cheer,
With every leap, they shed a tear.

The raccoon's hat is quite a sight,
Swiping snacks under starry night.
While a bear belly flops with glee,
His furry friends all shout, "Whee!"

Nature's stage, a grand affair,
Where laughter echoes through the air.
In wildwood realms, fun's the king,
Join the jesters, let joy take wing.

Tranquil Voices in the Birch

Two moose whisper, eyes a-glow,
Sharing secrets only they know.
Dancing leaves in playful drift,
As breezes play a gentle gift.

The rabbit wears a tiny hat,
While plotting how to catch a rat.
A hedgehog sings with quills in tow,
As mushrooms giggle, row by row.

All the trees join in the chat,
"Did you hear about the tiny cat?"
Squirrels snicker, roll in the grass,
As rabbits serve the punch in glass.

In birch trees' shade, the jokes unfold,
With every tale, their hearts are bold.
Nature's chorus, oh what a thrill,
Where laughter echoes, and time stands still.

Chronicles from the Canopy's Cover

High in the branches, birds exchange,
Tall tales of worms that taste quite strange.
A parrot squawks a pun with flair,
While monkeys swing without a care.

The sloth joins in, albeit slow,
"With all this chat, let's put on a show!"
The curtain's leaves begin to sway,
A talent night in wild array.

The frogs recite, while crickets play,
Their comic duo brightens the day.
Beneath the boughs, a crowd does cheer,
For storied antics they hold dear.

In the canopy, humor's crown,
Where laughter flows, it won't back down.
Chronicles shared beneath the green,
A tapestry of giggles seen.

Epiphany Under the Timbered Sky

Under the timbered arms, they meet,
Where laughter rings, and joy's a treat.
A deer wears glasses, looks so wise,
As fireflies flicker in the skies.

The porcupine has quite the style,
Sporting a tie, he walks a mile.
"I tell you jokes, that's my true art,"
He quips while twirling, quite the heart.

A fox runs by with cheesy puns,
While all the others share their runs.
In moonlit games, they play their part,
Creating joy from nature's heart.

Beneath the sky, the fun ignites,
In harmony, they reach new heights.
An epiphany in wooded grace,
Where every creature finds their place.

Lullabies of the Leafy Giants

In the shade where squirrels play,
A raccoon dreams the night away.
Whispers of leaves start to sing,
As the breeze drops by for a fling.

Bugs in tuxedos dance with ease,
Twirling 'round the busy trees.
A rabbit juggles acorns high,
While owls crack jokes as they fly.

Mice hold court with tiny cheer,
Sharing tales that all can hear.
Under stars, the laughter flows,
Pinching toes of sleepy crows.

So when you stroll past these bright views,
Remember the woodland's silly hues.
Each giant trunk, a story spun,
Life beneath them is just pure fun.

Chants Among the Woodland Giants

The trees croon tunes both loud and clear,
While chipmunks stomp and leaders cheer.
A lumberjack loses his hat,
Chased by a prankish little rat.

Dancing shadows, twirling around,
Ants in a line, perfect and sound.
Echoes of laughter fill the glade,
Where nature's humor can't be delayed.

Frogs take bets on who will leap,
While crickets giggle, not a peep.
Squirrels dressed in hats absurd,
Holding court with a clever word.

Join the fun, let worries cease,
In this grove of playful peace.
Beneath the giants' watchful eyes,
Life's little follies surely rise.

Shadows of Serenity

In the dusk, where shadows creep,
A turtle snores, while the ants leap.
Giggling ghosts of leaves above,
Whisper secrets, full of love.

The bumblebees buzz in delight,
Chasing fireflies into the night.
A hedgehog dons a tiny cape,
Pretending to be an escapee shape.

Every branch has tales to share,
Of all the critters caught unaware.
A raccoon claims the crown of thieves,
Snagging snacks from rustling leaves.

So let us bow to these old giants,
With hearts as light as springtime's clients.
For laughter rings in every breeze,
In shadows where the wild hearts tease.

Treetop Tales of Yore

Once a squirrel lost his nut,
He said, "Oh gosh!" and fell in a rut.
The wise old owl just rolled his eyes,
As laughter echoed through the skies.

A choir of frogs begins to croak,
While raccoons pull on silly jokes.
All the critters in a throng,
Join in singing nature's song.

A porcupine takes a brave stance,
Dressed in leaves, ready to dance.
Every twig has gossip to share,
As whispers flutter through the air.

Let's tip our hats to leafy towers,
Where giggles bloom like pretty flowers.
In this tapestry, joy's unfurled,
The fun and frolic of the woodland world.

Secrets of the Evergreen Grove

In the grove where secrets dwell,
Squirrels gossip, oh so well.
A robin sings of acorn theft,
While the wise owl takes a left.

Beneath the branches, shadows play,
Mice are dancing day by day.
A deer tells jokes to passing bees,
Frogs croak laughter in the breeze.

The whispers of the leaves at night,
Hold tales of mischief, pure delight.
The brook can't help but giggle loud,
As fawns prance, oh so proud.

Oh, the mischief in the air,
As critters plot without a care.
Imagining crowns made of sun,
Life's a jest, it's all in fun!

Songs of the Silent Sentinels

Under the watchful moon they sway,
Tall trees hum tunes that tease and play.
A squirrel dances with misplaced flair,
While raccoons argue who's the fairest there.

Chipmunks form a tiny band,
With acorns, twigs all close at hand.
They sing of snacks and hidden stash,
As shadows flit and crickets crash.

The trees, they laugh with every breeze,
At how the rabbits try to freeze.
Their ears gone cold, but still they dash,
For winter's coming oh, what a smash!

The sentinels stand, wise and grand,
Amused by antics, nature's band.
In harmony, they sway and sway,
As woodland creatures laugh away!

Beneath the Giant's Arms

In the shade of aged bark, they plot,
A gathering of woodland, never forgot.
Bears in bow ties, their style quite bold,
Tell tales of summers and winters cold.

Fox in glasses reads from a book,
All the forest folks steal a look.
While chipmunks flip for acorn cheer,
The laughter stretches far and near.

Beneath the giant's arms, they play,
With friendly battles all in jest today.
The trees remember every fabled jest,
As critters gather, feeling blessed.

In this realm where humor reigns,
Nonsense flows through the grassy lanes.
Nature's joy is woven tight,
In a tapestry of pure delight!

Lyrics Under the Leafy Vault

Underneath the leafy spread,
A hedgehog claims his cozy bed.
He strums his quills like a guitar,
Singing tunes of mischief near and far.

A party vibe with ants in ranks,
Pitches flip-flops, social pranks.
Badger skips with a cheeky grin,
While the fireflies join for a spin.

Each note echoes, playful and bright,
The forest sways with laughter's light.
A chorus of nature, wild and free,
Composing songs for you and me.

In whispers sweet, the stories flow,
Of critters grand and wild ego.
As daylight fades, the night takes flight,
Under the vault, everything feels right!

Syllables Beneath the Whispering Pines

Underneath the tall, green trees,
Squirrels chatter, doing as they please.
A raccoon wears a tiny hat,
As he stumbles on his trusty mat.

Mice tap dance in a little show,
While birds critique from the boughs, oh no!
Leaves rustle with laughter, what a sight,
Nature's jesters keep the mood so bright.

A frog croaks jokes, and the ants all cheer,
Crickets laugh, saying, "This is our year!"
A snail slides by, claiming he's so fast,
With a shell so shiny, he's quite the cast!

In this woodland, where fun is the fate,
Every creature knows it's never too late.
So gather 'round and join in the spree,
For silly sounds hide beneath every tree.

Shadows Dance in Verse

By the moonlight's gentle glance,
Shadows gather for a dance.
A squirrel wobbles on his toes,
While a hedgehog steals the show, who knows?

A fox in a cape does a spin,
While the owls all hoot, joining in.
Beneath the stars, they prance and leap,
The laughter echoes, deep to deep.

With twilight jokes and playful jests,
Each critter shows off their best quests.
A mole brings pie, though it's quite rare,
And the rabbits nibble without a care.

As dawn approaches, they start to fade,
Leaving whispers of the fun they've made.
But fear not, for when night resumes,
They'll reappear in the dancing blooms.

The Garden of Timeless Songs

In a garden where the flowers chat,
A bumblebee wears a sunny hat.
The daisies giggle in pastel hues,
While a daffodil tells the silliest news.

A worm croons tunes beneath the soil,
And the roses sway, embraced by toil.
Violets hum, as they peek and tease,
Like secret keepers on a gentle breeze.

The garden gnomes sit, counting their gold,
Trading puns, both brave and bold.
"What did the sunflower say to the moon?"
"Don't leaf me hanging, I'll be back soon!"

In this place where laughter blooms bright,
Nature's concert goes on through the night.
Forget your worries, come sing along,
In the garden of our timeless song.

Ballads of the Buckling Branches

Branches twist with tales of fun,
While the owls wink at everyone.
A raccoon strums on a moonlit lute,
Singing soft songs to a playful flute.

The wind joins in with a cheeky breeze,
Messing up nests, swaying the trees.
Squirrels argue who holds the crown,
As they chase each other up and down.

"What's the best snack for our little crew?"
A chipmunk squeaks, "It's acorn stew!"
And with that, giggles echo through the air,
As branches buckle, bending with flair.

From twilight's start until the day,
These lively critters come out to play.
With tunes and tales beneath the sun,
The forest sings, and we all join the fun!

Whimsy Amongst the Elder Trees

In a forest where the squirrels play,
The acorns dance and sway all day.
A rabbit's hat is quite the sight,
He says it's magic, oh what a fright!

Nearby a fox dons shoes of gold,
He struts around, so young, so bold.
The trees giggle as they hear him speak,
Chasing shadows, so fast, so sleek!

Verses of the Verdant Canopy

A bear in a tie sings a cheerful song,
With a chorus of birds, they can't go wrong.
The mushrooms nod in rhythm and glee,
Wishing they could dance like he!

In a nest up high, a squirrel does cheer,
For the nut he found right underneath here.
The giggles and chuckles keep swirling around,
In this playful realm, joy is found!

The Timbered Tales

An owl in specs reads stories aloud,
To a gathering of creatures, each one a crowd.
The raccoon pops popcorn, oh what a sight,
While the hedgehogs roll by on their bikes at night!

A deer dressed in stripes just can't sit still,
She's star of the show, with unstoppable thrill.
The laughter echoes through every branch,
As critters and trees join in the dance!

Sonnet of the Soaring Boughs

A sleepy sloth with dreams of flight,
Casts wishes on branches, oh what a sight!
The elf with a hat spins tales of delight,
Of cupcakes and cookies in the pale moonlight.

A raccoon juggles with apples so red,
While the birds just laugh, "Oh, what a spread!"
The trees whisper secrets to the ants below,
As giggles and joy through the forest flow!

Legend of the Leafy Giants

In the forest where tall trees sway,
Squirrels argue about who'll play.
One claims he's faster, the other's sly,
They race on branches, up to the sky.

A wise old owl gives a cheeky grin,
To the squirrels, he says, "Just let me in!"
"I'll judge your race, but don't be mad,
If you lose to me, it's not so bad!"

The rabbits laugh from their soft green beds,
As they munch on clovers with wiggly heads.
"Those squirrels think they're oh so grand,
But we're the ones who rule this land!"

With a wink and a hop, the laughter flows,
In this leafy realm, that's how it goes.
The giants watch, their branches sway,
As nature's jesters dance and play.

Love Letters to the Leafy Canopy

Oh, how the leaves whisper secrets above,
A beetle writes letters to the one he loves.
"Dear sweet vine, so twirly and fine,
Your tendrils wrap round me, oh, how divine!"

The critters gather 'neath sun's shining glow,
As a frisky chipmunk puts on a show.
"Dear tree, dear tree, I'm crazy for you,
Your bark is so strong, your shade is so true!"

A butterfly flutters, spreading her wings,
With dreams of romance and all of those things.
"To the branches high, I send my best wish,
For love grows here like a sprightly dish!"

And maybe one day, 'neath stars we'll find,
Leafy romances can make hearts unwind.
For all in the forest, love's never a bore,
Under the canopy, who could ask for more?

Starlit Meditations Among Roots

Under the moon, the critters gather round,
Mice in pajamas, beneath trees profound.
"Meditate here on the roots so wide,
And contemplate snacks we can find inside!"

Owls with glasses give wisdom on high,
"Remember to breathe, and never ask why!"
As fireflies flash, they light up the scene,
What's life without snacks? It's all quite routine!

The hedgehogs roll down the soft, grassy hill,
"With snacks and good pals, we've got all the thrill!"
They laugh at the turtles who take hours to stroll,
"We've all got our pace, let's just reach our goal!"

So under the stars, the friendships grow tight,
With tickles and giggles, it's sheer delight.
In this wooded nest, the nighttime feels right,
Bonding and bouncing till morning's first light.

Fables of the Forest Floor

Once a snail claimed his shell was the best,
"I can go anywhere, take a good rest!"
But a rabbit hopped by, and laughed in delight,
"I can bounce ten times before last night!"

Then a wise old tortoise joined in the fun,
"Slow down, quick folks, you've all just begun!"
"I may be slower, but I always win,
In the race of life, it's all about grin!"

A chipmunk popped up, with acorns galore,
"You may be quick, but I'm never a bore!"
"I've got the best snacks, let's all share a bite,
And forget about racing, let's party tonight!"

In the forest they laughed, with stories to tell,
Where creatures unite, and all friends do well.
With fables of joy, their hearts full of cheer,
Each morning returns, and so does the year!

Cadence of the Trunk and Bough

In the shade where critters play,
Squirrels dance, oh what a display!
With a wiggle and a jump they go,
Carrying acorns, putting on a show.

Frogs in tuxedos croak with glee,
Sharing jokes with a bumblebee.
A turtle wearing mismatched socks,
Offers wisdom that really rocks.

Mice tell tales of cheese so grand,
While ants march in a cheerful band.
Beneath the boughs, laughter and cheer,
A woodland party, let's raise a beer!

With every creak of branches high,
The giggles echo, oh me, oh my!
Nature's antics sparkle and shine,
In this woodland realm, all is divine.

Sylvan Serenades

Whimsical owls with glasses perched,
Hold midnight meetings, plans them searched.
While rabbits perform with hats and canes,
A jester frog entertains with refrains.

The wind whispers secrets, oh so hushed,
A chipmunk in a tie feels quite rushed.
As night unfolds, the laughter flows,
Underneath the stars, the magic glows.

Beetles dance on petals bright,
While fireflies twinkle throughout the night.
The symphony of giggles and screams,
Sings wildly in the land of dreams.

In the glade where shadows play,
A grinning fox leads the ballet.
With a leap and a bound, they all take flight,
In this forest of fun, everything's just right.

Mystic Melodies of the Woodlands

Beneath the trees where mischief brews,
Apples giggle in their fruity hues.
A hedgehog strums a leafy lyre,
Trading jokes around the bonfire.

Raccoons in masks, so sly and spry,
Debate the latest gossip and why.
The owls hoot with hearty cheer,
As dandelion fairies bring good beer.

The forest floor becomes a stage,
With every twig, their hearts engage.
Each ant's a dancer, each pine a star,
In this wild concert from afar.

Boozy mushrooms sway side to side,
While wise old trees nod with pride.
Together they weave a laughter spell,
In this woodland tale where all is well.

Harmonies from the Hollowed Roots

Under roots where giggles grow,
A snail's slow dance steals the show.
Nearby a skunk in stylish fluff,
Winks at the crowd, saying, "Enough!"

A bevy of birds chirp puns and quips,
While turtles recount their wild trips.
A mischievous breeze joins in the fun,
As mushrooms nod to the beat of the sun.

The flowers join in with petals bright,
Spinning tales of the moon's cool light.
Crickets strum their legs in glee,
Spreading joy with community.

As dusk settles in with a chuckle and cheer,
The fun of the forest rings in the ear.
In this merry grove where laughter erupts,
The happiness lingers, no one interrupts.

Folklore of the Forest Glen

In the woods where critters play,
Squirrels chatter night and day.
A raccoon once wore a hat,
Climbed a tree and fell flat!

The owls hoot with wise old glee,
While rabbits munch on clover tea.
A fox danced on a rock so round,
But tripped, and tumbled on the ground!

Through the ferns, a weasel darts,
With jokes that tickle forest hearts.
The trees shake with laughter, oh so loud,
While squirrels gather a giggling crowd!

So gather round, oh friends of mine,
Here in the glen, all things align.
With tales to tell and laughs to share,
Nature's jesters fill the air!

Murmurs of the Verdant Giants

Beneath the branches wide and tall,
The ants held a parade, oh what a ball!
With acorn hats and twiggy rides,
Marching 'neath the oak tree's sides.

The grasshoppers jumped in silly lines,
While fireflies twinkled like pocket designs.
A bear tried to dance on a log so grand,
But lost his balance—oh, wasn't it planned?

The wind whispered jokes through the leaves,
As the trees chuckled, pulling their sleeves.
One made a pun so silly and bright,
That even the shadows couldn't stop the light!

In the glen where giggles blend,
Nature's humor never will end.
So join the fun, let laughter bloom,
Where giants murmur, dispelling gloom!

Stanzas in the Shade of Green

In shady corners, whispers spill,
As critters gather for a chill.
A turtle told jokes, slow and grand,
While a hare tried to clap his hands!

The hedgehogs pricked up their ears,
As laughter echoed, banishing fears.
A porcupine danced without care,
Until he pricked a friend—oh, beware!

The trees leaned in, like they were guests,
Joking about who wore their best vests.
With laughter swirling in the breeze,
Even the flowers began to tease!

So come sit down upon the ground,
With friends, you'll find joys abound.
In the shade, let your heart be light,
With stanzas that make the day bright!

Ode to the Silent Wood

In a wood where whispers dwell,
A chipmunk stole a pine cone, oh so well!
He hid it from the curious crows,
But slipped on sap—now everyone knows!

A deer, with grace, tried to play hopscotch,
But ended up just looking like a botch.
The trees clapped their branches in delight,
As critters laughed into the night!

A wise old owl, with spectacles near,
Told tales of friends filled with cheer.
With stories spun from bark and pine,
Every critter felt divine!

So raise a toast to the silent glade,
Where laughter lives and worries fade.
In the wood, where fun never shies,
The spirit of joy forever flies!

Enchanted in the Evergreen

In a forest where squirrels wear hats,
And rabbits debate all the latest chitchats,
A deer plays chess with a wise ol' owl,
While foxes all gather to dance and howl.

The trees tell jokes in rustling leaves,
As pinecones drop down like sneaky thieves,
A bear with a tie munches on pie,
While the birds tweet gossip as they soar high.

Beneath branches thick, the laughter flows,
With acorns as popcorn for woodland shows,
A raccoon in tights takes the stage with flair,
Proving that fun can happen anywhere.

So gather your friends, bring your best cheer,
In this enchanted place filled with love and beer,
We'll toast to the trees, this wild, funny spree,
Forever we'll dance, just you wait, you'll see!

Legends in the Leafy Labyrinth

In a maze where the leaves form a vibrant mat,
A gnome with a beard chases after a cat,
The shadows weave tales of old, so bizarre,
With fairies on bicycles, racing afar.

The path twists and turns with a giggle or two,
As turtles in sunglasses strut on through,
A hedgehog recites poetry, slightly offbeat,
While we all share popcorn, a very odd treat.

Mysteries flutter like butterflies bright,
With whispers of legends that tickle the night,
A grumpy old troll plays the lute and sings,
Of love and mischief and tiny lost things.

So venture with laughter, step boldly and bold,
In this labyrinth green, where stories unfold,
With each twist and turn, we shall find our own muse,
In a world full of whims, for the fun we can choose!

Songs from the Sylvan Sanctuary

In the heart of the wood, where the sunbeams play,
A chipmunk writes music, "Oh, what a day!"
With a twig for a wand, and leaves as his notes,
He conjures up laughter, on tiny boats.

Harmonies drift while the fireflies rave,
As turtles join in, their shells all ablaze,
The frogs form a choir, quite comical too,
With rhythms of ribbits and splashes of dew.

The bunnies jump in, a tap dance grand,
While mushrooms bloom bright, like a touring band,
Around every corner, there's laughter to share,
In this sanctuary, with joy in the air.

So come as you are, bring your heart that's light,
For songs filled with giggles await in the night,
With nature in tune, oh, the fun we will see,
In this sylvan space, wild and always free!

Odes to the Old Ones

Here stand the ancients, their wisdom like gold,
With stories of wild days that never grow old,
A raccoon holds court by the gnarled old roots,
With judges of squirrels wearing regal suits.

Their laughter echoes in the branches above,
As they crack silly jokes like a warm hug of love,
An owl with spectacles reads from a tome,
Of mischief and mayhem, wherever they roam.

A bashful old tree, with knots all aglow,
Shares tales of the past—but wait, they're a show!
With pinecone confetti and laughs that ignite,
The joy of the ages, it sparkles with light.

So salute to the old ones, their wisdom we greet,
In the heart of the forest, where giggles compete,
With odes that resound through the branches so fair,
Embracing the laughter that dances in air!

The Enchanted Embrace of Oak

In a park where trees wear hats,
Squirrels juggle with tiny bats.
A raccoon sings for the crowd,
While owls hoot and feel quite proud.

The branches dance with a silly sway,
Leaves whisper secrets in a playful way.
Acorns fall like confetti bright,
Turning the ground into a delight.

Woodpeckers tap, like a drummer's beat,
While rabbits breakdance on tiny feet.
The ground is alive with laughter and glee,
In this whimsical place, wild and free.

At night, the moon joins the fun so dire,
Casting shadows that twist and require
A jig, a twirl, a jiggy jig,
The trees chuckle, and the stars do a gig!

Forest of Eternal Echoes

In a glade where echoes never tire,
A deer struts around like a funky choir.
Its antlers twirl, a regal crown,
While squirrels cheer, shaking hands down.

Each sound that bounces comes back with style,
A giggle, a chuckle, a perfectly timed smile.
The critters laugh, their joy is a gift,
As the trees sway, giving nature a lift.

Foxes throw a party, everyone's game,
Inviting in bears, with no sense of shame.
Hiccups of laughter burst from the deep,
As frogs start croaking their secrets to keep.

And when the dusk comes, all gather close,
Sharing tall tales and the newest boasts.
For in this place, where echoes reside,
Every sound carries joy, far and wide.

The Song of the Ancient Grove

In a grove where time seems to freeze,
A turtle waltzes with graceful ease.
While dancing ferns sway in delight,
As fireflies twirl, glowing in flight.

An ancient oak strums a leafy guitar,
Bunny backup dancers near and far.
Chirping crickets try to keep the beat,
As happy chipmunks shake their feet.

Each branch has a tale, a giggling sigh,
Of clever squirrels and owls up high.
The breeze carries jokes between the trees,
Making laughter dance like leaves in tease.

Beneath the branches, the spirits prance,
In a merry jig, they sway and dance.
Join the chorus of this woodland crew,
Where silly songs bring life anew!

Treetop Tales at Dusk

As dusk approaches, our stories unfold,
The tall trees whisper their truths so bold.
A parrot squawks, 'Have you heard the lore?'
'What kind of snack is best for a door?'

With each new rhyme, the branches sway,
While critters chimed in with witty play.
A hedgehog argues with a wise old crow,
About which one's the best at a show.

Moonlight glimmers, softening the boughs,
Bamboo beats give rise to raucous vows.
To celebrate life, we'll riddle and jest,
For in the treetops, we are all truly blessed.

Laughter echoes until stars align,
And all join in, as we sip on sunshine.
So gather 'round, share a giggle or two,
In treetop tales, so fresh and so new!

Dreaming Amongst the Giants

In a grove where shadows creep,
I found a snoring giant sleep.
His beard was tangled, full of sticks,
Awake he'd scare with mighty kicks.

I whispered dreams, oh so absurd,
Of sleeping bags and flying birds.
He chuckled deep, shook off the leaves,
Said, "Hush, or I'll take off your sleeves!"

Beneath him, squirrels played tag with grace,
While acorns fell like tiny space.
I laughed so hard, I dropped my snack,
He yawned, and sent it sailing back!

So here I lay, with laughter wide,
In my leafy friend, I find my pride.
Together we make quite the pair,
A giant and a dreamer, rare!

Ballads of the Burgeoning Branches

Under branches that twist and twine,
A squirrel sang, quite out of line.
"Hey, listen up, I'm quite the star!
My acorn songs go near and far!"

The birds chimed in with chirpy cheer,
"Your voice is sweet, but where's the beer?"
They danced around with all their glee,
While bees buzzed loud, "Let us be free!"

An owl hooted, wise and stout,
"Silence, please, this is a drought!"
But soon he joined their silly spree,
And laughed aloud, "I'm young like thee!"

The branches swayed with such delight,
As woodland friends sang all night.
Their ballads floated on the breeze,
While stars above winked with ease!

Nature's Lullaby in the Shade

In the shade where soft winds play,
A bear snores loudly, night and day.
I tiptoe past on padded feet,
Avoiding dreams of honey sweet!

A rabbit hops, its ears aflare,
"Shh! Don't wake him, he's a bear!"
The flowers giggle in the sun,
"Bear's deep sleep means more fun!"

With butterflies, we danced around,
Twisting, twirling, not a sound.
But then the bear began to grumble,
And down we fell, a silly jumble!

Nature's lullaby, a gentle tease,
In soft shakes, we bent the trees.
With every laugh beneath his snore,
We dreamt of mischief, evermore!

The Poetry of the Pine Breeze

In pine-scented whispers, secrets spin,
The breeze carries giggles, where to begin?
A chipmunk rapped on a hollow tree,
"Yo! This is my stage — just wait and see!"

A crow cawed loud, "You think you're slick?
Your rhymes are weak, you need a trick!"
With a flap and a flap, she jumped in line,
Together they crafted a beat divine!

The wind joined in, a playful song,
While the sun beamed bright, like all day long.
They wrote of mushy berries and cheese,
As laughter danced on the playful breeze!

Nature's poetry, a funny sight,
Creating music in pure delight.
So next time you stroll through the trees,
Listen closely to their witty pleas!

Chants of the Charmed Thicket

In a forest of giggles, the trees wear a grin,
Squirrels debate on who's fastest to win.
The hedgehogs dance, their quills all askew,
While rabbits do yoga, in bright shades of blue.

Birds sing with glee, in a comical choir,
A lizard runs schemes that inspire a fire.
The mushrooms are chatting, albeit quite low,
They gossip and chuckle, as only they know.

Epic of the Sunlit Glade

Amidst the tall grasses, a party unfolds,
Where ants wear top hats and secrets are told.
The sunbeams perform, like jolly old fools,
While frogs leap for joy, breaking all of the rules.

A flower starts waltzing, with petals so bright,
Laughing with daisies, what a wonderful sight!
The laughter of critters rings out with delight,
As the day rolls on, filled with giggles and light.

Woven Stories of the Woodland

In the shade of a tree, a spider narrates,
Tales of the squirrel who conquered his fates.
The owl sits diligently, wearing a tie,
Presiding over fables that make the winds sigh.

The raccoons are plotting their next snack attack,
While foxes are role-playing, dressed in all black.
The laughter rolls on like a river in spring,
As nature unites, in a festival fling.

Birth of a Thousand Murmurs

A breeze carries whispers, both silly and sweet,
As the turtles debate if they'll ever compete.
A beetle starts tickling a slumbering snail,
While ants in a line follow a comical trail.

The wind chimes in, making music with glee,
As the leaves join in with a rustling spree.
With laughter like sunshine, the day dances through,
Painting smiles on the petals with colors anew.

Ballads in the Bristlecone

In the forest, trees wear hats,
Singing songs like silly cats.
Squirrels dance, but oh, they trip,
Chasing dreams, then take a dip.

Old pine trees crack jokes all day,
Branching out in their own way.
Laughing bark and wiggle roots,
While the fox dons squeaky boots.

Woodpeckers join a tap dance crew,
Bongo beats to entertain you.
Bristlecone with wobbly glee,
Who knew trees could dance so free?

Every whisper brings a grin,
Nature's circus wears a pin.
Come and join the leafy play,
Where trees and critters joke all day.

Tides of Time in Twilight Woods

Twilight's glow brings giggles near,
The owls hoot, 'Drink a cold beer!'
Frogs recite their limerick tales,
While fireflies light up like sails.

A turtle slips on a slick log,
And lands with a great big fog.
The raccoons make a grand parade,
In mismatched socks, they're unafraid.

Mossy paths whisper 'come and play,'
As shadows dance in the delay.
Time rolls on like a slippery fish,
With laughter echoing every wish.

Dancing shadows 'neath the moon,
Even skunks hum a funny tune.
In these woods, with jokes we climb,
We'll stand in awe of silly time.

Whispers in the Woods

In the woods, the whispers tease,
Secrets shared among the trees.
Birch trees gossip, saying 'Hi!',
As the squirrels pass by, oh my!

A hedgehog tells a corny joke,
While rabbits laugh 'til they choke.
Squirrels flick their fluffy tails,
When acorns start to spin like sails.

Deer hold a fashion show in grass,
With dandelions, a trendy class.
Wandering foxes wear bright coats,
And serenade the croaking goats.

Every rustle brings delight,
The woods are filled with purest light.
Join the fun, it's a grand affair,
Where laughter blooms in fragrant air.

Evergreen Eulogies

In the pines, they share their tales,
Of falling branches, broken nails.
With giggles that echo trees' height,
They ponder lumberjacks at night.

The saplings poke fun at the old,
'You're too slow, you've turned to gold!'
Wind whispers secrets with a grin,
While nature's show is set to spin.

Bumblebees buzz in harmony,
Creating tunes from bark, so free.
They giggle at the clouds up high,
"Why so fluffy? Come down, oh my!"

Each twig and leaf join in the song,
With laughter loud and joys so strong.
In this grove of chuckles and cheer,
The evergreens spread fun every year.

Songs of the Timeless Timber

In the woods so vast and wide,
Squirrels dance and cats divide.
A rabbit sings a silly cheer,
While foxes roll and disappear.

The trees all giggle, sway, and creak,
Whispering secrets, oh so sleek.
A bear wears shoes; he takes a jog,
And trips right over a sleepy frog.

The owls nod off, no time for hoot,
As turtles stock up on tasty fruit.
The sun peeks through with a golden smile,
While ants throw parties, all in style.

So gather close, let laughter rise,
As whispers spark, and truth defies.
In this realm where shadows meet,
Life's a dance on tiny feet.

Secrets from the Skyward Boughs

High above in leafy crowns,
A parrot wears the silliest gowns.
It sings of socks and lost car keys,
While giggling winds tickle the leaves.

Chipmunks trade their acorn snacks,
While squirrels point and make wise cracks.
A raccoon with a top hat says,
"Join my waltz in the moon's warm rays!"

A sloth on branch, forever still,
Practices poses for a thrill.
He yawns and grins, takes his sweet time,
For what's a moment without a rhyme?

So listen close to the branches sway,
As laughter spills in the light of day.
The secrets sung from above so bright,
Are whispers of joy in the golden light.

Murmurs in the Forest Shade

In shadows deep where stories play,
The mushrooms chat and children sway.
A lizard wears a tiny tie,
And grins at bees that buzz nearby.

The flowers gossip, their colors gleam,
While toads croak loud to the bubbling stream.
A hedgehog prances, proud and round,
With jokes about the earth below the ground.

The wind, a friend of cheeky pranks,
Rustles leaves and steals our thanks.
A scarecrow snickers, "I'm not just straw,
I'm the finest dancer, see my draw!"

So wander here, enjoy the tease,
Among the trees, life's sure to please.
In murmurs sweet, let laughter flow,
Amidst the shade where joy can grow.

Verses in the Verdant Vale

In valleys green where giggles sprout,
The rabbits race and tumble about.
A turtle plays the banjo low,
While dancing daisies put on a show.

The birds throw notes like frisbees high,
As butterflies flutter and pirouette by.
A snail with shades is looking cool,
Takes a slow lap around the pool.

The sun winks down on this merry pack,
As shadows join in the playful act.
A dancing mushroom wiggles bright,
Inviting all to join in the light.

So gather round, and let joy sway,
In every verse, let laughter play.
In this vale where fun abounds,
Is the best of all the silly sounds.